Peggy

Peggy

Peggy Urmston

CONTENTS

PEGGY - THE EARLY YEARS vii
PEGGY ix

1 Peggy - The early years 1
2 2 2
3 My Granddad 5
4 Wallington and Frater 8
5 Jubilee Day 1935 13
6 King George V 15
7 Living in Frater Lane 16
8 1939 - War is Looming 19
9 Back to 1931 22
10 Better Times 25
11 January 1940 27
12 Bombing in London 30
13 Girl Guides 34
14 Leaving School & Being a Parlour Maid 36
15 Factory Life 38
16 Nursemaid 42

| VI | —

EDITOR'S NOTE 44

PEGGY - THE EARLY YEARS

PEGGY

Peggy - The early years

Peggy Urmston - her early years

Born in 1927 in Trinity Street, Fareham, these are her memories of her early life, in her own words.

2

Peggy
1931 - 1932

It was an awful long way from the railway station in Fareham to Granny's house in Trinity Street. My first memory is of being carried the last few steps on my mother's hip. This was the house of my birth three years earlier. The house was number 28 of a terrace of identical houses. Front room and kitchen, stairs up to two bedrooms, there was one cold water tap outside the back door for the use of three houses. In the winder the tap would freeze up and had to be defrosted with the use of a page of burning newspaper. To me, this was a great magical thing.

In Granny's house there was a man sitting by the kitchen range and a lovely ginger cat. The man was my Granddad and the cat's name was Ginger. I don't remember anything for of my Granddad until he died, not so long after that. I remember his coffin on trestles in the front room. My Aunty Phyllis was only four years older than me, so we spent lots of our childhood together. When Granddad's coffin was in the front room, Phyllis was lifted up by Granny to say goodbye to him. I cried bitterly because I wasn't lifted up too.

That first day that we arrived, Phyllis and I were put to bed by my Mum and Granny and after a kiss from both of them, we settled down to sleep. I was only three years old and everything was so strange. I started to cry for 'my Granny', the one in Wales, my paternal Gran. Granny came up and said "What's the matter, my little chick?"

I sobbed and said "I want my Granny."

She said, "I am your Granny," and gave me a cuddle. With that I settled down and from that day I had no memory of my time in Wales.

Across the back yard was the wash-house which contained a huge copper for the laundry with a fire underneath for heating the water. My Granddad in Fareham had been a taxi driver and after he died, Granny took in washing from the gentry of that area to make a living for herself and for Phyllis who was only seven years old. I remember how hot and steamy it was all day with load after load of washing. Granny then had to hang it out to dry in the garden, iron it all and then walk back to the owners with great piles of washing in her arms.

The wash-house was quite big and in later years it made an ideal playroom for me and my friends on rainy days.

Mum and I lived with Granny for a time until my Dad came home from India where he served in the army. He left England just before I was born so he had never seen me. When he arrived I said, 'You are not my Daddy. My Daddy is a soldier.' (He was not in uniform so I didn't know him s Daddy). This was not a good beginning, I am afraid because he apparently thought my Mother had taken a lover in his absence. It all caused quite a bother.

In the course of time, my sister Gwen was born. My Dad absolutely worshipped her. All her life she could do no wrong in his eyes so therefore she became very spoilt. Everything she wanted was to be hers. I know that I became very jealous of her especially as I had to take her with me everywhere I went when out to play with my friends. This made life very difficult for me in my teens when I became interested in boyfriends. When going to the cinema she blackmailed me into giving her my sweet ration (It was wartime by now so we only had a few sweets anyway) so as not to tell on me.

At five years old when starting school, the teacher asked my name. I said 'Peggy Price'. She said 'that is not a proper name, ask your mother when you get home.' This upset me as I thought I haven't got a name. Of course my mother then told me that I was christened Margaret but she had shortened it to Peggy because it was common to call Margarets Maggy which she considered to be an ugly name.

I loved my school days at that school and was very happy there. After school most days I went home to Granny's house with Phyllis, to see her before going to my own home. I seem to have spent lots of time there and I had many friends who lived nearby. One of my friends, June Limborne was my friend right up until adulthood and even after we both married, but as time passed we both moved to different areas and so gradually lost touch.

Phyllis was my Aunty, being my Mother's younger sister. As a child it was a mystery to me how another child could be my Aunt. All my other aunts were grown up. In the next pages I will tell what I know of my forebears.

3

My Granddad

My Granddad
My Grandad's name was Samuel Simpson and he was born in a cottage near the Delme Arms. It was in a small row of cottages as you go under the Delme railway viaduct in Fareham. He had a brother called David who married Emily. There was also a sister called Edith (My Great Aunty Edie) who was married to Bert. They had two children, Gordon and Geraldine. David and Emily had a daughter called Nellie.

Samuel married Alice Churcher so they became my Granny and Granddad. Their children were my Uncle Jack, my Mother, Dora, known as Dolly, and much later came Phyllis after Jack and Dolly were adults. Alice Churcher, my Granny, had a sister Annie, who after married lived in Portsmouth, also another sister, Edith. There were other members of the family who emigrated to New Zealand in the early 1920s so I have no knowledge of them.

My father was Idris Price who was born in 6 Thompson Villas, Ynysybwl near Pontypridd in Wales. He was one of many brothers and sisters who I never knew except Uncle Billy, again a much younger late addition to the family. My Welsh Granny apparently did not speak English, only Welsh, therefore my first language was Welsh. Sadly it was all forgotten on my return to Fareham.

My father had a very hard early life, leaving school at the age of 12 years, then went down the mines, the only work in the village that all the men did, getting up before light and working until dark. I don't know how they did its but they were all wonderful singers.

Dad left the mines as soon as he was old enough to join the army. There he met and became great friends with my Uncle Jack. They were both stationed at one of the forts, either Fort Fareham, or Fort Wallington, one of the forts surrounding Portsdown Hill. From this friendship my Father met my Mother and before long they were married. Soon after they were married my Father and Uncle Jack were both sent to India for 4 years. Then my Mother took me as a small baby to live with my Granny in Wales.

Going to school as a child was a pleasure, the first home with both my parents was in Wallington, so we walked from the house, over the bridge of the river Wallington, up the hill to the High Street, across the main road to St. Peter and St. Paul Church with the school opposite. Being a church school, we spent a lot of time in church. One day, (a special saints day I presume) we went to church in the morning and then we were given the rest of the day off. I didn't want to go home so spent the rest of the day wandering about until I thought it was home time. I think I was the only child to play truant from home. The main reason I was reluctant to go home was that I didn't want to be made to look after my small sister Gwen which it seemed to me to be my main job at home.

Going to school one winter's day it was freezing cold and on the way I found an ivy leaf covered in thick ice and as I lifted the leaf away from the ice I had a perfect ice leaf. All the veins of the leaf were shaping the ice in a perfect t match. I took it to school to show to my teacher which led to an impromptu lesson on nature and the formation of ice from rain in freezing temperatures. It must have been a very cold day for it not to have melted as soon as I touched it, but I don't recall feeling cold.

One day at school we were asked to bring a bunch of wild flowers to school. There was to be a competition for the best bunch. I went out into the meadows and collected a bunch of three different colours to make an artistic type posy. I thought it was very beautiful and proudly took it to school next day. I noticed all of the other children had mixed flowers of all kinds which I thought looked very untidy. I didn't win.

The idea was to find as many different flowers as possible. The prize was a drawing book. Later in the day teacher called me into the staff room. All the teachers were there. On the table was a drawing book and a packet of crayons. They said 'you made a very beautiful posy and think you should have a present. Which would you like, the book or the crayons?'

I said 'I would like the crayons please. I can always find some paper to draw on but I don't have any crayons.'

I was so happy and I don't to this day know why they did that. I suppose they saw how disappointed I was, but at the end of it all I had the better present.

4

Wallington and Frater

Wallington

In Wallington, we lived in Drift Road - number 6 The Mount (Drift Road). This road led up to the old fort in Wallington. It was derelict by this time and all covered in grass like a meadow. It made a lovely place to wander and there were loads of brambles growing there. In late summer we, my Mum and other friends would take baskets and bags and pick blackberries to make into puddings and jams.

I remember my Auntie Edie and my cousin Gordon staying with us for the summer holidays so Gordon and I spent most of the time adventuring together in the meadows and lanes of Wallington (Gwen tagging on of course).

Dad used to make home made dandelion wine and Gordon and I decided to pick some dandelions for him. We had just bought a lollipop each and after eating them I put the lolly stick in my pocket. Scrambling up the bank at the roadside to pick some dandelions, I slipped and somehow the lolly stick came through the cloth of my pocket and stabbed me in my knee, whereupon it broke off leaving only a small part still sticking out of my leg. I couldn't pull it out and neither could Gordon. Along came a couple on a motor-bike with sidecar and stopped to see what was the matter. They couldn't pull it out either. They then decided to take me home in the sidecar, leaving Gordon to walk back. Dad couldn't pull it out Doctor we go, me in the sidecar, Dad on the back of the motor-bike. Doctor Kersop lived on the High Street in Fareham. It wasn't surgery time but he saw me anyway. He had a great struggle and finally went to his garage and came back with a pair of pliers. At last, success...

Back to school next day, excused P.T. and allowed to sit in the classroom at playtime for a few days. I was about eight years old at this time, and Gordon was six. Today we would never go out so far alone. It is a sad work we live in, children today never know the freedom and innocence of our days.

At number one The Mount lived Mr and Mrs Murphy with their three sons, Billie, Johnny and baby Herbert. All of us children played happily together. One of our favourite playgrounds was the old tannery on the other side of the river Wallington. It was rather a dangerous place to play because there were the remains of the deep vats, wide open, surrounded by brick walls which we dared each other to walk across. Luckily we had no fear and were very sure-footed and never had a fall. Beyond the tannery were the open meadows, in the summer, full of wild flowers - meadowsweet, cornflowers, buttercups and many others. We would sometimes take a bottle of home made lemonade and some sandwiches and have a picnic on the grass, and not come home until late in the afternoon.

At the corner of Drift Road was a public house with its own brewery. Sometimes Mrs. Murphy would make some home made bread. For this she would sent me with a large jug and a penny to the brewery to buy some yeast. I would return with a foaming jug full of yeast all ready to tip into the flour mix in a large china bowl. I recall that this bowl was the same one she used to soak baby Herbert's nappies in... My Mum always refused the kind offer of some of the bread. I wonder why?

At the brewery sometimes the workers would allow us children to explore inside and watch the process of beer brewing, until the manager came in one day and stopped us coming in. He said it was too dangerous and so it probably was.

The river was also a lovely place to play. We would take a jam jar on a piece of string and catch toddlers to take home. They never lived very long in the jam jars and then we would have a burial in the garden.

On Sundays Gwen and I were sent to Sunday school and on Mothering Sunday we went to church and were each given a bunch of violets to take home to Mum. I remember on Palm Sunday, we were given a cross made of palm to commemorate Jesus' ride on a donkey into Jerusalem. The people had spread the palm leaves before the donkey for him to ride across. Of course, I had never seen a palm tree and I couldn't understand the palm cross. My imagination saw leaves of oak or other trees that I knew. It was only years later that I realised the cross was made from fronds of palm leaves.

Sometimes on Sundays we would go with Phyllis to the cemetery to visit Granddad's grave. We would pick some Ox eye daisies that were growing wild in the hedgerow and put them in a jam jar on the grave. After that we would play in the cemetery in between the graves and jumping over them. We were told off, of course, by the other visitors to the cemetery.

We always seemed to spend a lot of time at Granny's house and I remember well her delicious dinners. Rolly Poly Pudding with bacon inside as a main course, and sometimes faggots and peas. Also fish and chips from Jack's fish shop further up Trinity Street. Granny would sometimes make a summer pudding for sweet, but more than often it would be rice pudding. I have never tasted a better rice pudding since.

On rainy days, Phyllis and I would play in Granny's bedroom. She had a lovely feather bed with iron railings at the head and foot. We would play at being angels by standing on top of the rails and 'flying' down onto the feather bed! It was great fun.

Every summer there was a Sunday school outing. Phyllis and the other older children were taken on the ferry to the Isle of Wight for the day. Us younger children were taken on the train to Hayling Island. It was such a happy day. The beach was lovely and sandy ('the seaside') as opposed to Lee-on-the-Solent and Stokes Bay which were mostly shingle. (That was just 'going to the beach'). When we were young we were taken there by our parents on an open top bus. When we were older, eleven years old, Gordon and I were trusted to take Gwen by ourselves. We liked that better, all that freedom from parents to do as we liked all day. It could never happen today.

When I was 10 years old my parents decided to move. We went to live in Frater Lane, Elson. I was very unhappy to go. I thought I would never see Granny again - it was such a long way on the bus. It also meant getting used to a new school and meeting new children. It was not nice being the 'new girl'. However, we soon settled down and made lots of new friends.

Whilst we still lived in Wallington, we would, on a Saturday, take a trip to Portsmouth to shop at Charlotte Street Market. Sometimes as a special treat, Mum would take us on the bus the 'pretty way', which meant a long ride into the country via Wickham, Boarhunt, Southwick and over Portsdown Hill through Cosham, North End, and so on to Commercial Road. At the Guildhall in Portsmouth was a small park with an aviary where we used to walk. Nearby was Verrecchia's Ice Cream shop. Mum and dad would have a huge ice cream wafer you could hardly get your mouth around and Gwe and I would have a cornet each. They were the biggest cornets in the World.

Afterwards we would go on to the market where we could buy almost anything. Mum would buy lots of fruit and vegetables. Our favourites in season were pomegranates; they took ages to eat as we picked out all the seeds which were very sweet.

After we'd moved to Frater Lane to live, we would still go to Charlotte Street Market but by the alternative route. A bus ride from Frater Lane down to Gosport Ferry. It was lovely on the boat - it was a steam boat and it had an observation platform, to the engine room where we would stand and watch the pistons going up and dow. There was a lovely smell of the fire and steam. When we reached the Portsmouth side there was a long walk up the pier If it was low tide we would look down onto the mud flats where the 'Mud Larks', local boys, would be standing up to their knees in mud. "Throw us a penny", they would call and sometimes Dad would throw one down and the boys would dig in the mud up to their elbows to find it.

Jubilee Day 1935

Jubilee Day

In 1935 when we still lived in Wallington, we celebrated Jubilee Day. This was the 25th anniversary of the reign of King George V and Queen Mary. The children had a day off school and we were each given a Jubilee mug. That day there was a fancy dress parade all through Fareham ending in a large field just beyond the top of Wallington Hill. I remember we stood at the top of the hill just opposite the old post office to watch it go by. It was very jolly with lots of bands playing at intervals along the routes. It was a very hot day and suddenly there was a terrific thunderstorm. We all became very wet but we didn't care, we were having such fun. We followed the procession to the field where there was a fun fair and lots of games and competitions.

My Granny had a lovely book - blue with silver writing on the cover. It was full of pictures of the royal family from the time of Queen Victoria up until the present day. About a year after this the King died and we then looked forward to the next king. This should of course, have been the current Prince of Wales but there was a problem - he was in love with an American lady - divorced. It was decided that he could not be the king and also marry Mrs. Simpson. He, of course, chose the path of love and abdicated.

There was a little ditty we children used to sing:
"Look who's coming down the street,
Mrs. Simpson, Who is she?
She's the one who stole our King.

Don't you think that's an awful thing,
Oh, me, oh, my..."

This was sung to the tune of the ukulele player, George Formby who was a very popular entertainer of the day.

6

King George V

The New King

In 1937 King George VI came to the throne with Queen Elizabeth. They had two little girls: Elizabeth and Margaret. We children loved the two princesses because they were about the same age as us. We thought they were so pretty in their lovely dresses. Again, for the coronation day all the younger children were given a mug, and the older ones a lovely book, very like the one for the Jubilee two years earlier. By this time I was old enough to have one of these books and I cherished it for year. It finally became lost during the war years.

7

Living in Frater Lane

Frater Lane, Gosport.

At the bottom end of Frater Lane was a meadow which led down to the shore of the inner Portsmouth Harbour where we children went to play. Crossing the meadow was a railway line with a level crossing manned by a guard who we called "Penny on the railway". He let us play in his signal box and showed us how the levers worked and told us about this line. It was private, belonging to the Admiralty and was used to carry goods from one shipyard to another. It was closed on Sundays and one Sunday we decided to take a ride on the trolley up and dow the line, just like in a Laurel and Hardy film. It was very naughty but we never did get found out.

One day, playing on the seashore, we climbed into a rowing boat anchored to the shore and played with the rope of the anchor. After a while, the anchor came loose and my friend said, "see that big ship out there, my Father works on it, let's row out to see him."

So off we went, quite a long way, and then her Father saw us. He jumped from the ship and swam out to us, climbed on boar our boat, furious with us. He said, "don't you know the tide is flowing out, you can never row back again. I will have to row you."

After him rowing for quite a long time, he said "I will have to go back to the ship - you will have to row very hard to get yourselves back to shore."

So now we were on our own and beginning to feel very frightened. By now, somehow our parents had been alerted. I supposed by the other children on the shore. There were several of them waiting and wondering what to do. Then a big boy, I suppose about 16 years old, came out and rescued us. By this time the tide was right out and we had to walk across acres of black mud to reach the shore.

I was wearing a white dress that day and by the time we reached shore we were both covered with smelly black mud. I don't know if it was that which made Mum angry, or the fact that we had frightened her half to death! I can't remember being punished but I suppose we must have been.

My Uncle Jack was a regular soldier and spent most of his service abroad. After 4 years in India with my Father, he then was sent to Singapore by which time soldiers were allowed to have their wives with them, so my Aunty Ivy went with him. They had four children, David, Eileen, Jean and Heather. By the time we lived in Frater Lane they had all returned to live in married quarters somewhere near North End in Portsmouth.

We often went to visit them there and may Uncle Jack always greeted me with a big hug and kiss and called me his favourite niece. Of course, I was his only niece until Gwen was born, but I didn't think of that. When they were abroad he always sent me letters and pretty foreign cards. He was my hero.

At Christmas time Gwen and I were invited to the children's Christmas Party at the NAAFI canteen. There seemed to be hundreds of children in the great hall with a Christmas tree as high as the ceiling. We played lots of games, musical chairs, pass the parcel, and many others. Then it was tea time - jelly and blancmange, tinned fruits and lots of cakes with orange squash to drink. After tea Father Christmas arrived and we all had a lovely present. I was given a beautiful humming top, all colours which blended together as it spun. Gwen's gift was a very pretty fairy doll. We all wore party dresses that day; mine was a lovely turquoise colour with small pleated edging around the neck, sleeves and skirt in a lovely shiny material.

After the party we all went home with Uncle Jack and Aunty Ivy and our cousins to stay for the rest of the weekend, sharing beds with the children.

8

1939 - War is Looming

1939 - 1941

War is looming

The village school at Elson was not far from Frater Lane and Gwen and I walked there every day. Gwen was only five years old then and I was ten. It was a very nice school and had nice teachers. I was there for one year and then at eleven years old I went to Brockhurst School for Girls.

One day, the head mistress came to the first year class to find the youngest girl in the school. That just happened to be me. The Lady Mayoress was coming that afternoon and they wanted me to present her with a bouquet of flowers. They took me to the staff room to learn my lines. "Will you please accept this from the staff and scholars of Brockhurst School."

I learned then that I had not sounded the "L" at the end of will. They trained me to say it properly. Then I was sent home at lunch time to put on a clean dress. When I returned I was examined to see if I looked smart and could say my piece properly. Later in the afternoon, the Mayoress arrived and I had to mount the stage and present her with the flowers. I was very nervous in front of the whole school.

During that first year every one was anticipating the probability of a war with Germany. There was talk of all the children being evacuated as we lived so close to the naval establishments. When the parents were asked to give all their children's names, my Mother refused to let Gwen and I go.

Then it was August, and my Father, being in the reserves for the Army, was called up. He left home on the 15th to go to Arborfield Barracks in Berkshire. Mum took us girls for a holiday visit to my Aunty Edie and Uncle Bert who lived in West Norwood in London. Gwen and I had a lovely time with Gordon and Geraldine, our cousins, going to the park each day to play. Sometimes we were taken to Brixton, the nearest shopping centre and occasionally up to the City. We saw Nelson's Column and the Houses of Parliament and went on the river by boat.

One Sunday we were all playing in the park when suddenly the air-raid sirens started up. All the barrage balloons were rising up into the sky and we children were watching them in fascination. A lady came hurrying by and said, "you children had better hurry home, your parents will be worried about you." We thought we had better do as we were told but we couldn't think why. As we were walking back there was lots of activity in the streets with air-raid wardens rushing about. One of them grabbed us children and took us into a big hall. We hadn't our own gas masks with us so someone found us some. We were very bewildered and beginning to feel worried.

After a while, Uncle Bert came rushing in to look for us and took us home. He said, "the war has started and there is an air-raid on". We arrived at the house to find Mum and Auntie Edie and Gordon's grown up sister, all rushing about and arranging the kitchen table into a sort of tent with jugs of water at hand, and lots of tinned food lined up. To my surprise, there was even a chamber pot and a bucket. After all that, it turned out that the air-raid was a false alarm. So - that was the beginning of the second world war.

The next day Mum took us back home to Frater Lane and then we found that all the schools were closed and all the children apart from us had been evacuated. I never saw any of my friends again.

As my father was an older soldier, he was on the staff at Arbofield, hopefully for the duration of the war. Because of this, and the fact that it was away from the coast and therefore a safer place to live, my father first of all found rooms where my mother could live whilst looking for a cottage for all of us. In the meantime, Gwen and I went back to Fareham to live with Granny and Phyllis.

9

Back to 1931

Back to 1931

I now go back in time to when my Father came back from India in 1931. At this time there was very high unemployment and Dad was often out of work. Times were very hard for Mum and Dad to make ends meet. Mum would go to work as a maid to some of the large houses in Fareham and Granny would have the care of Gwen and me. No doubt despondency caused Dad to go to the pub more often than he should and Mum became very unhappy.

One day, when Dad came home from the pub, she said, "that's enough. I'm leaving you!" She then took Gwen in the pram and with me holding her hand, we walked out of the house. I remember we went down the road together as far as Wallington Bridge and then turned around and went back home. There were many tears and then Dad said, "Right I won't take another drop." And nor he did until my Christine's wedding day in 1969, and then only one glass of beer.

I was fast learning to read and write at school and Dad would get me to read to him out of the newspaper, mainly the sports page. I would read the football results and he would do the football pools - he never won an money though. It took me many years to realise he had never learned to read or write. All he could do was sign his own name. I think now that perhaps he was dyslexic - such a thing was never heard of at that time. All I knew was that he was very bright in other ways and was great fun to be with. He was always singing to us in the style of Paul Robson, very often making up his own words to the song.

We had a wireless set that ran on 'wet batteries' and every so often I took the dead battery for recharging at the village shop. I had to carry it very carefully so as not to spill the acid from it. I don't know why it was called a wireless because Dad took a long piece of wire from the wireless right out in the garden and string from the top of the two clothes posts as high as he could get it. At that time we had no electricity, only gas-light or candles.

As we were so poor, we didn't have a Christmas tree until we went to live at Elson in Fratton Lane, but we did have Christmas presents, Father Christmas never forgot to visit. I was always given my favourite books and I remember Gwen had dolls and dolls prams and such-like presents. Dolls never interested me very much.

I do, though, remember coveting a doll that sat in the post office window at the top of Wallington Hill. Every day as I went to school, I would stop at the window and gaze at the doll. At home, Mum used to put money on the mantlepiece to pay the rent, or insurance man, or for tradesmen who called weekly. There was a two shilling piece sitting there for several days for one of these people. The temptation was so great, it was exactly the price of the doll. I stole it.

As I was passing the post office, I walked in to buy the doll. What happened? I couldn't bring myself to ask for it, instead I bought a small doll costing only one penny.

"That's an awful lot of money you have," said the lady in the shop as she gave me one shilling and eleven pence in change. It was a lot of money in those days as weekly wages were often no more that two or three pounds.

What to do with all this change? I gave pennies to m friends in class and teacher noticed. She asked where I got it from. I told her it was a present.

It was a terrible thing I did. When I got home, my Mum was in tears and frantic about the lost money. Of course she found out that I had taken it, I was so ashamed and so I am still. I shall never forget it.

10

Better Times

Better times

At last my Father found some regular employment in the building trade, but it was in Elson so that is why we moved to live in Frater Lane. Our lives then became richer, we children had better clothing and more things like birthday parties and a Christmas tree for the very first time. I remember having 'proper' school clothing consisting of a gym slip and blouse to start school in the Seniors at 11 years old. I was so pleased with myself.

At this school I found a very good friend, Doris Hart. She was older than myself and who used to come to my house to play. Sometimes Mum and Dad would go out and leave us at home for a while. "Stay indoors and don't open the door for anyone," they would say. Doris would arrive and we were no allowed to open the door for her - what to do? We opened the window and she climbed in to be with us. We never told Mum and Dad and we thought it was a great secret.

We had a lovely cat at this time and when we all went for a walk on a Sunday, she would come with us. Sometimes it was a very long walk and before we arrived back one os us would have too pick her up and carry her the rest of the way as she was so tired.

One day, Dad brought home a puppy for us; he was a lovely dog we called "Boy".

When he was still a puppy I was playing with him and holding him in my arms when suddenly he slipped from my grasp and fell to the floor. Mum was out working so she gave me some money to take him to the vet because he was limping badly. The vet lived in Gosport so I took him on the bus because Gosport was quite some way from Frater Lane. We saw the vet who said the puppy was fine, it was just a sprain. After leaving the vet I went to the bus stop and climbed onto the bus. I suddenly realised the bus was not going back to Frater Lane, but on towards Gosport Ferry. The bus conductor was very kind. He told me to stay on the bus as it would turn around at the Ferry to return to Frater Lane. Only then did I realise that traffic always drives on the left and I stupidly got on the bus at the same stop that I had got off, silly me.

11

January 1940

January 1940

Gwen and I are now living with Granny in Fareham and at the beginning of the school term I started at the Fareham Senior school. I arrived in the classroom and teacher asked me if I knew any of the girls. I didn't think that I did but then one of the girls put her hand up and said she knew me. It was June Lisburn and we hadn't seen each other since I went to Frater Lane to live. There was an empty seat at her desk so I was told to sit with her. I was so pleased.

Now because of the war starting, I had missed a whole school term and when it came to arithmetic I was all behind and was unable to catch up. Long division was a close book to me and I just had no idea what to do, June helped me a lot and I sometimes copied her book. Then the teacher found out and I was moved to another desk. The decimal points system was also a great mystery but I managed to grasp it eventually. Because of this I was unhappy at this school but had great times with June. We invented a secret code and would write notes to each other.

Luckily for me, by Easter time Mum and Dad had found a house to live in at Binfield so we were all together again in Berkshire, well away from the fear of bombings.

Binfield was a lovely village near Bracknell, very quiet and right in the heart of the country. The village school was about one mile from our house, and each day Gwen and I would walk to school. We took a pack of sandwiches for lunch and stayed there all day. It was a lovely friendly school and I was surprised at how full it was. I later found out that it was because half of the children were evacuees from London. When I arrived the children asked which part of London I was from. They were very surprised when I said I was from near Portsmouth. Was I bombed out? They wanted to know. The only thing I was unhappy about was the fact that only the boys had art class and the girls had needlework which at that time I found very boring. None-the-less I persevered at it and to my surprise I won second prize at the end of the school exams. I was sorry not to be allowed to join the art class though.

At one time at school there was a competition for anyone to make and paint a wartime poster. Of course all the boys were expected to enter, so I asked teacher if I could have a go. She was very doubtful about this but in the end he allowed it. So I made a poster. It was displayed with all the others, but of course I didn't win a prize. The other girls thought I was very strange.

June and I still wrote coded letters to each other, right up to the end of the war and after. I made a lot of friends at that school. The ones I remember best were Sybil Green, Beryl Busby, Veronica Hanon and Kathy Cain. Veronica was physically disabled but she knew ballroom dancing. She had a gramophone and we would play it in her garden and she taught us to waltz, the quickstep, all the old-time dances, the Valletta and the tango. At school we also learned country dancing.

Sybill was the expert at needlework and she always won first prize for sewing. Kathy was an evacuee from London and she always met the postman and asked, "have you got one from my Mum?"

Beryl's parent owned the village laundry and at the back of the house they had an enormous garden with old outhouses that we all loved to play in. They also had a walnut tree and it was great harvesting it in the Autumn.

In needlework lesson, all the girls made themselves an apron to wear in cookery class. Being a small village school there were no kitchen for us to practice in. Every Wednesday we travelled in a school bus to another village, taking with us all the ingredients for that day's lesson. We were taught how to weigh the flour and all ingredients on scales, but we also learned how to measure by cups and spoons as it was not everyone in those days who owned such a thing as kitchen scales. I remember making short crust pastry which can be used for fruit tarts or meat or savoury pies.

One day we made bread rolls, but most of them were so hard we threw them at each other on the bus on the way back. Mum was not amused because all food was on ration and it was very hard for her to spare enough coupons for the ingredients.

We all had our own ration books with coupons which were exchanged for butter, cheese, meat and eggs, all dated for use each week of the year. It was impossible to buy and fruit or vegetables that did not grow in England.

The hardest thing for us children was the fact that sweets were also rationed so it was a great treat at the end of the week to take our sweet coupons to chose our sweets, then Mum would share them out in small batches for each day. Sometimes we would eat them all at once and then it was a very long wait until the next week.

We had some rhubarb in the garden and Mum made some jam with it. It wasn't very nice because we didn't have enough sugar to make it set so it was very runny on the bread. We ate it anyway.

12

Bombing in London

Bombing in London

The bombing raids in London were getting very intense and at night we could hear the noise and see the glow in the sky from the explosions. It must have been terrible. For us to be able to see and hear the raids, about 30 miles from London. Before long, my Aunty Edie and cousins Gordon and Geraldine left London and came to live with us. Uncle Bert had to stay in London because he worked in the newspaper office but he came down at the weekends. It was very much of a squash as we only had two bedrooms.

All four of us had to share a bed - Gwen, Geraldine and I slept at one end and Gordon at the foot. The cramped conditions led to many a quarrel between us before we finally went to sleep - each complaining that the other one or more had their feet or elbow in one's face.

Mum and Aunty Edie shared the other bed. When Uncle Bert and Dad came home at the weekends, Uncle Bert and Aunty Edie stayed with another family along the road but sometimes made a bed on the floor of the front room.

Gordon and Geraldine then came to school with us, but after a few days I heard the Headmaster say "I can't teach this boy anything, he has already passed even the top class in his knowledge." Gordon had by then sat his eleven plus exam in London and shortly after he came to us he was told he had won a scholarship to Dulwich College. That meant that he had to return to London to take up his place. He just came down to us with his Dad at the weekends after that.

From time to time, as the bombing raids eased off, Aunty Edie went back to London and left Geraldine with us. I don't wonder at it as it must have been terrible for Aunty knowing her husband and son both had to stay there, and of course Geraldine was just a very little girl to be separated from her family.

We were very lucky to be in Binfield away from it all, but one night we were all suddenly woken up by a series of terrible bangs which shook the house. A bomber had flown across and released his bombs all over our village. It was thought that he was escaping the barrage of gunfire from London and dropped his bombs anywhere in his flight.

The next day as we walked to school we passed where one of the bombs had dropped. One house was badly damaged but luckily no-one was killed, only minor injuries. This was the first time any of us had seen the results of a bombing raid and suddenly we realised just what was happening in London and other large cities near the coast. From time to time, we had more stray bombs but they only fell into meadows and fields around us.

During the summer that first year of the war, we suddenly found to our delight there was a fair arrived at the village. At the bottom of the hill in Forest Road, there was a pub with a huge hollow oak tree in the large green area on the fork of the road and a country lane. This oak tree laid to claim that it was a hiding place to King Charles. It was on this green area that we found the fair.

We had a lovely time spending our pocket money on the various attractions. It was a very small affair with swing-boats, a roundabout and a hoopla stall. We thought it would be there for a few days and we would all go there each day. After a time we found it stayed there for week after week. We realised that it was staying because it had nowhere else to go with there being a war on. Now I understand that it was such a small fair because it just belonged to one man all on his own. He would 'man' the roundabout by turning a wheel by hand own the inner circle of it.

We children could use the swing-boats on our own with just a helping push from him to start it swinging and the hoopla stall he could watch at the same time as looking after the roundabout. From time to time, he would let us have a free ride. I think that he must have been quite lonely.

About a hundred yards further along from the fair, was the river. In the heat of the summer, my friends and I would go to play in the water. Always there were several other children from the village and we all had a great time. On the right side of the bridge the water was very deep and we never played there - it was far too dangerous. As the water passed under the bridge, it met a weir so by the time it reached the left hand side, it was more shallow. A few yards downstream was a very small waterfall and beyond that it was shallow enough to paddle up to our waist. This was the favourite place for us all as we could pretend to swim with one foot on the bottom. Most of us couldn't swim, but those that could would go in above the waterfall and have a lovely swim. There were a lot of catcalls from those, daring us non-swimmers to join them. We had too much sense to take notice of them, although we did envy them non-the-less. As it was wartime and even clothing was on coupons, very few of us had swimsuits so we went in in our knickers. This was all very well for the boys, but some of us girls were beginning to show signs of puberty with little breasts beginning to show. This did not deter us from enjoying the river, most of us didn't seem to notice, and if we did, we were not bothered.

If we followed this road and then turned right, we would eventually come to the small town of Bracknell. At that time, it consisted of one main street with a cinema, a few shops and a library. Once a week Mum would take us to the pictures to see the film that was on. Each week was a new film. The show consisted of a short minor film followed by the news reel, followed at last by the main feature. After that we all stood to 'God Save the King' and then out.

We walked all the way home again. There were some buses, but sometimes we had to wait for a whole hour for one to come along. Sometimes the film show ended a little early and then we managed to catch an earlier bus home. We were very happy with that because it was quite a long way to walk.

13

Girl Guides

Girl Guides

There was a girl guide meeting in our village and my friend, Beryl, persuaded me to join them. Each week we met in the village hall and sometimes in the summer, in the Captain's house. It was a large house with a huge garden to have our meeting out of doors.

As it was wartime it was not possible for us to go camping so we had a day in the recreation ground to learn camping skills. We were taught how to light a camp fire with only one match and then one of each group made a meal for four people on the fire. I made a meal of sausages and mash, followed by a chocolate blancmange! For this I won a cookery bade to sew on my uniform. There were many other badges to be won, some girls had so many, they covered their whole sleeve. I managed to get six. Quite a few of the badges available were for sports activities and I am afraid I was never very athletic. My badges were for First Aid, Nursing, and other domestic issues. My yearning was always to be a nurse when I was old enough, so naturally my first badges were for First Aid and Nursing.

On the 11th November every year we joined the church parade for Remembrance Day, marching along behind the band of the other groups, Home Guard, Land Army Girls, Boy Scouts, Army Cadets, and any other groups of war workers. One year it was very cold with about a foot of snow, so we had to march in wellington boots. By the time we reached the church, about one mile, our feet were very cold indeed. It was particularly sad for us in Binfield that year, as six months before, one of the young girls had been married in this church to a young soldier . Only six weeks after this, he had been killed in action, so his name was read out in church along with others who had lost their lives in the war.

By now we were into the third year of the war and we were seeing more and more soldiers about, sometimes on manoeuvres, along the village street. Walking through the village to school one day, the roadway looked different and strange to us children. As we drew nearer, we realised there was a long row of tanks and armoured cars with soldiers all under camouflage netting. To our surprise we found they were all American. They were not like our English soldiers, their uniforms were much smarter looking, the cloth of the uniforms were smoother and a much nicer shade of khaki. The boots they were wearing were very quiet, not hob-nailed as our own soldiers, so you hardly hear them when they marched along. The other wonder to us children was the fact that they all had chocolate and chewing gum that they gave us as we passed them by.

14

Leaving School & Being a Parlour Maid

By now it was the end of July. I would be 14 in August which meant I would have to leave school at the end of term. As my father was a serving soldier my mother was entitled to a family allowance until I left school. I asked her if I could stay on for another term, so she saw the headmaster to see if this could be arranged. As I had missed a whole term at the beginning of the war, he said it would be a good thing to do. I was very pleased about this so after August I went back to school for another term.

Half way through that term my mother heard of a job that she decided would be just right for me, it was to be a house parlour-maid in a big house in the village. I begged her to let me stay on at school until Christmas but she insisted I took up this post. It was a living-in post so that meant I had all my meals provided, and my bed, so Mum didn't have to feed me any more.

I earned ten shillings a week and out of that I had to give Mum seven shillings and six pence, leaving me with two shillings and six pence for myself.

I HATED IT!

I was up at six in the morning to light the fire in the drawing room and dining room and then clean the floors and polish the furniture before Madam and Sir came down to breakfast. Cook came with me to make the beds after breakfast and showed me how to clean the bathroom. I had never seen one before. At home it was just a tub in front of the fire.

I then cleaned the bedrooms and set the dining table for lunch. Cook showed me how to set the cutlery properly and which glasses to use, and how the place them properly. It was quite an education for me. I helped cook to prepare vegetables for lunch and for the evening meal. After we had washed up after lunch, we rested in the kitchen for an hour, then it was time to make the tea and take it to the drawing room at four o'clock.

Dinner was at eight o'clock and I served the evening meal. Madam taught me how to serve, always from the left and to take the dirty plates from the right. I quite liked this part of the job and learning how to do it helped me quite a lot in later life.

In the evening, cook and I sat in the kitchen after we had tidied the dining room and washed the dishes, but I was expected to be at the call of Madam if she wanted anything. At ten o'clock cook said I could go to bed as Madam would not need me any more. So off I went, snivelling, because I was so unhappy.

Every day was much the same but cook asked me if I went to church on Sundays. I had to say I didn't go very often so I was told that if I did I could have time off to go to church. Silly me, I should have said yes and then I could go and see my friends. I was allowed a half day off each week to go home and to see friends. I told my mum how unhappy I was there so at the end of the month I left and went back home.

15

Factory Life

Factory life

There was a factory in Bracknell where they made white Blanco for cleaning tennis shoes and also khaki Blanco for soldiers putties. These were a sort of short gaiters that reached from the top of the boots and the end of the trousers were tucked into the tops. They reached up to the lower part of the calf.

In another part of the factory was made tailor's crayons, these were either triangular or square-shaped. In yet another section where one had to wear face masks, there were lots of sheets of brown paper. This was spread out on the floor and sprayed with a nicotine solution (hence the face-masks), then put through a shredder. This was them added to pure tobacco to bulk it out a bit. Don't forget, there was a war on so most things we consumed had some kind of additives to make them go further.

After leaving service at the big house, I went to work in the factory. Mum didn't like this one bit as she had the old-fashioned idea that nice girls didn't do factory work.

By this time I had acquired a bicycle so I could ride to work. In the morning I started out before daylight to reach the factory at first light. Being wartime, it was important to use as much of the short winter days so as not to waste electricity. By the same token, we stopped work at 4.00pm. This was called "Daylight Saving". The clocks were set on

British Summertime in the winter instead of Greenwich Meantime, and in the summer were put on double Summertime.

My first days at the factory I was put to work on the assembly line for packing the white Blanco into individual packets and then into boxes of dozens. It was quite jolly - the other girls and women were very friendly and there was music all day for us to sing to, "Music While you Work", on the radio. We stopped for tea-breaks during the day and took sandwiches for lunch. In the summer we sat outside in the car for our breaks but in the winter, we stayed in the workshop.

To make the work less monotonous, we changed round after a few weeks to the khaki benches. All the Blanco blocks were made from the same mixes except for the colours. The men did the actual mixing, then the more qualified women worked on the presses that made the blocks. Strangely, there were different patterns for different manufacturers but all came from the same mix.

After a while, I was transferred to the section that made tailor's crayons. It was more interesting for me because there were different colours and shapes to work with. This time I was packing the individual crayons into boxes. They had to be packed very carefully between tissue paper as they were quite delicate and would break very easily. Because of this there were quite a number of rejects. Occasionally I would put one of these rejects into my pocket to take home as I liked to do colouring and drawing in my spare time,.

Of course factory work paid better wages than domestic work, so I had more pocket money for myself and I could also give Mum more. The other advantage for me was that I had evenings free so could once again join my friends in the evening. We still went to Veronica's house to play the gramophone and to practice the dance steps.

On Saturday evenings there was always a dance held in the village hall, so we went to it quite regularly. We usually danced together as the boys were too shy to join in. It was usual for the girls to sit or stand on one side of the hall and the boys on the other side. There we would watch each other, hoping that one of the boys would be brave enough to come across and ask one of us to dance.

There was always a refreshment bar at one end of the hall which served beer for the adults and soft drinks for the young people. It was not easy for us to sneak a glass of beer because everyone in the village knew just how old we were. At ten o'clock on the dot, by Mother expected me back home so that meant I had to leave the hall before the dance had finished. This I resented because all the others stayed to the end and then walked home together. Sometimes my Dad would come to the hall to collect me if he had the weekend leave from the barracks.

After several months at the factory, I heard of another factory at Wokingham which paid more money than the one at Bracknell. This on was for war work where we made batteries for aircraft. They came in all sizes from the smallest torch batteries to quite huge ones, about 12 inches square.

Again the work was on assembly lines where all the various components were put together, then filled with pitch. One day I was distracted momentarily as we were chatting and pick up a battery that still contained hot pitch. This tipped up and ran over my fingers. I had huge blister over two of my fingers - gosh didn't that hurt! I was always much more careful after that.

After the batteries were completed they were then taken to the paint shop to be sprayed with airforce grey paint. For a while, I worked in the paint shop spraying with a great spray gun into an area full of batteries. I had to wear a face mask for this job as the paint was very toxic. We were only allowed to work in there for short periods of time and then return to the assembly lines.

During the war there was a group called "The Girls' Brigade". It was sort of a grown up Girl Guides. The forewoman started up this group in the factory so lots of us young ones joined it. For uniform we wore nave blue skirts and white blouses, We used to meet once a week and did lots of things together like knitting or sewing and playing games together. It was quite fun to belong to and it gave us something to do in our spare time. Of course, we also went on church parade on special days.

16

Nursemaid

Nursemaid
I worked at this factory for several months until I heard of a job in the village as a nursemaid. This was the sort of job I would love to do as I was still too young to do hospital nursing.

It was lovely working with two little boys. Nicolas was three years old and Robert was ten months old. I suppose really I was more of a mother's help to start with as Mrs. Luke was working with me for bathing and dressing the boys and I also did a bit of house parlourmaid work as well. They had moved down from London; they had a house in the village. Mr. Luke worked in London and he only came home at weekends.

I slept in the same room as the boys and in the morning Mrs. Luke and I dressed the boys and gave them breakfast., After breakfast the boys went into the garden to play with Robert sitting in a playpen. Then I helped with the housework. There was a woman who came each day to do the rough work and also some cooking. After lunch I changed into my nursemaid uniform and took the children out for a walk in the village for an hour or two.

We used to have the bombers coming over and when that happened, we had to get out of bed - the children stayed in bed but we got out of bed and stood against the inner walls of the house because we were told that was the safest place, which, if you can imagine if a bomb came down it would hit the outer walls and we would be safe if we stayed by the inner walls. So this is what we did - we'd be standing there. I must have got out of bed too quickly one night because I wasn't standing there for many moments when I fainted, fell down and Mrs. Luke was in a panic because the nursemaid had fallen down in a faint. I was maybe fifteen by then.

Children left school at fourteen in those days, unless they went to the high school and I was never bright enough to do that.

We went away to stay at somebody else's house for the week for Christmas. At tea one day, there we all were, all the children with paper hats on. I was sitting at a small table with a little boy next to me, he was leaning over the table with his paper hat on. There was a lit candle on the table. I thought to myself, any minute now that hat is going to catch alight - but I sat and watched it happen. I was naughty, watching. I could see it was going to happen. I remember thinking any minute now that candle is going to catch his hat. As it caught fire, I pounced on it, I got it in time and was the hero of the hour! I could have prevented it happening.

I loved working with that family. Mrs. Luke saw me drawing one day. I drew pictures of the children's teddy and panda and hung them on each side of the fireplace in the nursery. 'Oh,' she said when she saw them, ' we shall have to get you some art lessons in the village. A teacher came and was booked to give me six lessons. Then the teacher said that if I could find someone else in the village to join in, she would do us both for the same price. A young lad from up the road then joined in. So then there were the two of us having drawing classes in the kitchen of the house. This went on for quite some time and I still have all the paintings I made at that time. She also gave me a book of Vincent Van Gogh paintings.

EDITOR'S NOTE

Mum kept that book of Van Gogh paintings and it inspired her to keep doing her own paintings. As an adult she continued making lovely pictures with pastels too, and later stitched many tapestries.

Mum always wanted to be a nurse, and in 1946, the war over, and at 18 years old, she did begin training in London. Unfortunately she didn't complete the course at that time, but moved back home to her parents in Fareham. It was around this time that she met and fell in love with a young Polish Soldier, Alfons, who had arrived in England at the end of the war. It wasn't long before they married and in 1948 Peggy's first child was born, a little boy she named Peter. I believe she felt her life was complete at that moment and not long afterwards, in 1950, I was born. My younger brother, Stephen, was born in 1953.

We lived in a brand new council house on an estate in North Fareham. Life was good, although we were poor, as most people were in the years following the war.

It wasn't until all three of her children were at school, that Mum began working in the local psychiatric hospital, Knowle Hospital, near Fareham, as a nursing assistant. She finally achieved her aim to be a qualified mental nurse in 1961.

In Mum's later years, she travelled far and wide with her second husband, John, spending many months each winter living in a camping van, exploring Morocco, Spain, France and Greece, amongst others.

Now 98 years old, Mum lives in Hartwell Lodge Care Home in Kiln Road, Fareham, just one street away from where she was born in Trinity Street, all those years ago. She still enjoys drawing and painting and often slips into the mode of Ward Sister when she is interacting with the other residents and even tells the staff off.

I love to visit Mum in the care home. She is happy and the team there are very caring with all the residents. A big thank you goes to them all.